Letter 2: What Is Right and Wrong?

by Leonard Swidler, PhD

About iPubCloud.com

iPubCloud.com is the Digital Publishing arm of iPub Global Connection, LLC. Focusing on globally transformative books from authors all over the world, we value and help promote the works of creators who influence our world in matters of equality, interfaith dialogue, psychology, philosophy, and planet sustainability.

Our value to you is simplicity and convenience. The continually curated book list is culled from the New York Times, Amazon reader reviews and iPub subject matter advisors. You may be confident when you select an item from our store; everything is fulfilled by Amazon, its affiliates, and other important distribution channels.

There are many books like this one on iPubCloud.com along with selections of other categories of books. Don't keep us a secret. Connect with us on Facebook and join our mailing list. And, if you have a story to tell, reach out.

iPub Global Connection, LLC
http://www.iPubCloud.com
550 W. Baseline Rd., #303
Mesa, AZ 85210
info@iPubCloud.com

Cover Design by Arewa Abiodun Ibrahim
Cover Image by Axel Bueckert/shutterstock.com
ISBN 978-1-948575-14-0 Paperback
ISBN 978-1-948575-15-7 Kindle

Contents

Introduction

"Will" is short for Willow Athena Swidler-Notte, my fantastic grand-daughter, born at the beginning of the Third Millennium (2000), to whose house I have been going practically every weekend since 2011, to teach her German (which is why I am addressed as *Opa*, a typical German abbreviation for Grandpa), and slowly talk about all kinds of interesting things in life—and end up having a vegetarian dinner with Will and my brilliant daughter Eva and her wonderful husband Ian (both are professors, Ian high school ecology/biology, and Eva university history).

These are my letters to Will, with whom—when you meet her, you will understand why—I clearly am madly in love.

Opa,

Len Swidler, (*info@ipubcloud.com*)

How Do We Know What is Right and Wrong?

1. Don't Take Things for Granted

Dear Will,

After my last letter to you, you wrote back and asked, "what is right and wrong?" and how do we know them? Again, you ask simple, and therefore hard, questions! When I say "simple" questions, I mean those that touch on the deep underlying ideas about what it means to be human. Those are the things that we tend to take for granted. But to take something for granted can trip us up very badly! It is those "taken for granted" matters that philosophers spend their whole lives thinking about. Let me give you an example, Will, of something that we humans just take for granted and never, or hardly ever, think about or ask ourselves questions about.

Example: We just assume that things our senses present us are really the way we perceive them. But have you ever stuck a straight stick in clear water? What did you see? It looked like the stick bent very sharply in the water. But when you pulled it out, it was straight again! Well, that raises the question, "Can we believe the evidence of our eyes?" To put it another way, we often have to start wearing glasses when we get much older. When we don't wear them, everything looks a little blurry—but everything is just as sharp-edged now as it was before out eyesight began to weaken!

Will, when you first looked at a drop of "clear" water under your dad's microscope, you were shocked to see all those little critters swimming around in that "clear" water. And remember when you began to read about atoms for your science project, you learned that the nucleus is about as big as a tiny fly flitting in the center of a huge cathedral, the walls of which are like the first ring of electrons. Wow! That means that the very building blocks of all matter are mostly not "matter," but just "space," like between the tiny fly and the cathedral walls! So, if we were able to slip something—it would have to be very super tiny—between the electron and nucleus we would find—"nothing"! That means that the block of iron that seems so solid to our hand is mostly …. "nothing"?

About now, Will, you are doubtless beginning to ask yourself: Where is Opa[1] going with all this!? What I want to stress is that what we, without thinking about it, just take for granted often turns out to be something quite different, or at least is much more complicated than we "assumed!"

---

[1] Opa is a German abbreviation for *Grossvater* (Grandfather), sort of like "Grandpa."

2. Meaning of Ethics and Morality

So, Will, let's start by getting clear about two words that are usually used in this area of "right and wrong." In English, there are two words we usually use: "moral" and "ethical." Some contemporary thinkers try to make a distinction between the two terms, but in the process, they only show their ignorance of Latin and Greek. Will, you have heard me say numerous times how important it is to study Greek and, even more, Latin if you want to have a good grasp of English—because almost all the so-called "higher" terms in English come to us from Latin and Greek, frequently through French. You, Will, know perfectly well from your omnivorous reading that the Norsemen conquered and settled in northwestern France, gave it its name, "Normandy," and from there also conquered England (1066 C.E.), bringing with them their French language—and England's royal road to the huge, rich Latin language and its ideas!

It happens, Will, that "moral" comes from the Latin *moris*, and means "custom," whereas "ethical" comes

from the Greek *ethike*, and means—surprise!—
"custom"! So, "morality" and "ethics" and related
forms of those two words mean basically the same
thing in English! Ah, yes, you probably are thinking
that when somebody does something cruel to
another, they are called "immoral," but if someone
cheats in business, they probably are called
"unethical." You've got that right! However, this is
just custom (I hope you got my clever pun here
about "custom"—awe come on, Will, you have to let
your Opa have a little word fun!).

OK, so what do we mean when we say that
something is right, good, moral, ethical, or wrong,
bad, immoral, unethical? I hope you remember
the basics of our earlier discussion in my first
letter on what we mean when we say something
is "good" or "bad." Recall, we agreed that we said
that something is "good" because it reached what
we understood as it's "goal" or "purpose" that we
had in our head. Remember, Will, we used as the
first example ice cream, and that we would call it
good if it did what we thought the "purpose" of

ice cream was—that is, to be cool, sweet, creamy.... Well, basically the same thing operates here, only in ethics and morality we usually are talking about, not so much *things* like ice cream, but about *actions*. So, for example, we might say that lying is *im*moral or *un*ethical because we think that purpose of the action "speaking" is to transfer the thought we have in our minds to someone else by either the spoken or written word. But a lie defeats the "purpose" of communicating what is in my mind to you! Hence, we call a lie, bad, immoral, unethical.

OK, we now have the basic meaning of the key terms that we use when talking about right and wrong fundamentally clear. I hope, Will, that you are beginning to notice that getting a clear understanding of basic terms gives us something solid to build on as we tackle more complicated things. Our past discussion about good and bad gave us a solid starting point for further discussion here of right and wrong, ethics and morality.

3. How Do We Decide Whether an Action Is Good or Bad?

Well, Will, you doubtless are now asking yourself, how do we know that some action reaches its "purpose" or not, and hence is good or bad, right or wrong? It is easy enough to figure out what the purpose is of ice cream or Mozart's music—as we spoke about them in our first letter—but a lot of people tell all sorts of lies, for example. How come, you are thinking, they don't know that such action is contrary to the "purpose" of talking, that is, saying what is in our minds?

Will, you are onto exactly the right question: How do we know what the purpose of something is and, therefore, that following it out will be good, right, and not doing so will be bad, wrong? We could take a stab at trying to answer now the question about this or that specific action, but I would like to suggest that we start with the "foundational" ethical question. In other words, I would again like to go back to our initial question in our first letter, the meaning of life. What! We first have to answer the biggest question of all, the whole meaning of human life?! Now relax, Will, I don't mean that we have to solve that huge question here and now (if we really *could* clearly solve it now, we should immediately rush into print, for people have been working on it for thousands of years, and have come up with a number of very different, not always compatible answers). Rather, I mean that we should look just *broadly* at what role the various answers to that overall question play in the more *specific* questions that we are raising here about how we come to know that some action is right or wrong.

Will, we noticed earlier in our first letter that, when a baby is born, its mind is to a very large extent like a blank slate (*tabula rasa* in Latin), and that our experiences write on that slate, and over the years slowly make us into thinking, self-aware human beings. As this happens to us, we begin to ask ourselves the big question that you asked in your first letter—does life have meaning and, if so, what is it? What I want to strongly suggest,

Will, is that that broad answer will be the general "location" where we will stand, and then from there decide whether this particular action fits into the overall "purpose" we have decided life has—or not. Think of it this way, if you decide that the purpose of life is to gain and enjoy the maximum amount of wealth, then you may say to yourself that to lie or steal to gain and enjoy more wealth is ethically right, even though others may have a different position. You just don't want to get caught stealing or lying. Why? Because that would run counter to your "purpose" of gaining and enjoying ever more wealth—because having to pay a huge fine, or to go to prison would make you lose wealth or prevent you from enjoying it and, hence, would be counterproductive to your overall "purpose" in life: Gaining and enjoying the maximum amount of wealth.

Well, Will, now you are probably either rather puzzled or very eager to get the "answer" to the meaning of life. I suspect that you are not very much the latter—eager to know *the* answer to the meaning of life—because through your huge amount of reading you already realize that there are lots of people who have very different answers to that big question, which probably makes you doubtful about there being *the* answer that everybody agrees on—because there isn't one! Some people, for example, think that if you follow a bunch of essential rules of living, you will go to Paradise or Heaven when you die, and if you don't, you will go to Hell. That was a very widespread belief, but an awful lot of people did not and do not hold that position. Some people think that there is a kind of life after the grave and some don't. So, Will, you are probably beginning to think, Yikes! Is it all total chaos?

If, however, you think about the question a little, you will recall that in the thousands of books you have read, there really are an awful lot of actions that most people would agree are fundamentally good, ethical, and moral. I am sure, Will, that you could name several obvious examples right away—like, say, not hurting or killing another innocent person, or not taking things that belong to others, not deliberately giving wrong directions to someone asking for directions, not being mean to others.... I am sure you could continue this set of examples that you and most everyone else would say are wrong, are immoral. Fine, but the underlying question you asked—and it is an extremely important one, Will—is, how did you, and I, and other people get to know that they were wrong?

4. The Golden Rule

Perhaps the most basic principle of ethics that we see at work here, Will, is the so-called Golden Rule. It comes in both negative form: "Do not do to others what you would not want them to do to you"; and in positive form: "Treat others as you would want them to treat you." I am sure you have often heard and read it in one form or another because almost all the ethical systems humans ever devised have it at the very center of all their rules. We find it way back at the beginning of the great systematic ethical thinkers like Zoroaster, Confucius, Lao Tzu, the Buddha, the ancient Greeks, the Hebrew Bible—all roughly around 500 B.C.E.

When you think about this principle, you begin to realize that it's not just helpful in making people kinder and more pleasant to be around. No, Will, think a bit more deeply about it. If everybody went about treating all others in ways that we did *not* want to be treated—including basic things like lying, hurting and killing—everybody would bashing and stealing from each other. It would be like the "War of all against all!" that the famous eighteenth-century English philosopher, Thomas Hobbes, said the human condition was like in the beginning millennia of human existence. And yes, we now know that is the way it was to a large extent for thousands and thousands of years, for all the ancient skeletons of twenty, fifty, one, two hundred thousand years ago that we have discovered in the last three hundred years all show signs of having been violently killed! Think about it, Will! For scores of thousands of years, our ancestors in effect made no progress at all! Until, at most, twelve thousand years ago, when our ancestors were all still hunter/gatherers. Fortunately, after the invention of farming (as noted in my first letter, most likely by women!) twelve thousand or so years ago, eventually enough people got together and set up a leadership structure and then the leader worked to stop the stealing and killing—think of Hammurabi of 1700 B.C.E. and his famous laws. Why would a leader try to stop the stealing and killing? You can answer that easily—because if his farmers and animal herders stole and killed each other, the leader, say, the king, would get fewer taxes! So, he in effect said: "Stop killing my farmers and herders, you're destroying my taxes!"

You may be thinking, Will, that that is a very self-centered position to propose as the foundation of all ethics! Aha! Remember, we brought up precisely this issue when in our first letter we talked about the destructive notion of "extreme dualism," "body bad, spirit good," and that we were often taught that we should suppress our "ego," our "self"? We saw that the first thing we love—that is, that we want to unite with the "good," be it ice cream, Mozart's music, friends….—is our own Self, our own Ego. The expression of the Golden Rule that we have from the Bible says it clearly: "You should love your neighbor *as* you love your self"! That little word *as*, Will, is the key. Remember, we talked about the importance of not shrinking, but of expanding our Self, our *Ego*—even to the point of making others *Alter Ego*s, Other Selfs. We saw that this was not our "giving up" good things, but in the long run our gaining more and more good things, for increasingly the "good" is being brought together not just with my relatively small *Primus* [first] *Ego*, but with my ever-expanding *Alter Ego*—siblings, friends, neighbors, city, country, world....

So, OK, now we at least have a beginning of a foundation for deciding what is right and wrong, namely, the Golden Rule: Don't do the things to others you would not want done to you. Actually, the way the Hebrew Bible and Jesus, among others, expressed it—positively—is even more helpful, for it urges us not just to avoid doing harmful things to others, but to actually do positive things to others that we would wish they would do for us. For example, Will, if you could not swim and somehow fell into the Schuylkill River and were about to drown, and a strong swimmer, George Kelly, came jogging by and saw you, you would want George to stop running and jump in and save you. Now reverse the situation: you are the strong swimmer jogging by and George Kelly can't swim and is drowning. I'm sure that you would say, "Of course, not only would I stop and save him, but also that I *should* stop and save him because I would want him to save me!" See, Will, you have just made a general ethical rule for yourself! I should do everything for others that I would want them to do for me if our situations were exchanged! That is how the great ethical thinkers of the past came up with the Golden Rule.

5. The Global Ethic

About twenty-five years ago, a couple of us thinkers in this field of ethics and all the different systems that have been developed over the centuries (some are called religions and some philosophies) came up with the idea that we call the *Global Ethic*. For the sake of full disclosure, I have to say that, of the two thinkers, one is my very good friend from Germany, Hans Küng, who I have known for almost sixty years! He is very famous, doubtless the most famous theologian alive today, in 2018. The other thinker is me, your Opa—not so famous!

What Hans and I did was to dig even deeper than we had since we started our university studies of ethics in the 1940s (yes, right at the end of World War II, in 1946). We started with doubled intensity after the end of another very big war, the Cold War (1945-1989). Hans wrote a small book, *Weltethos*, which you recognize, Will, means a "World Ethic." The term I used in English was a *Global Ethic*. This was an approach that was very different from the hugely violent efforts of global ideologies that dominated the world over the previous century; I am talking about Fascism (Italy/Spain), Nazism (Germany), Imperialism (Japan), Communism (Russia), Maoism (China). They all tried to force their "meaning of life," and their accompanying ethics, first on their own people, and then on the rest of the world. The fight against them, Will, took up most of Opa's adult life. They are all either gone now or are at most only a fading shadow of their former super powerful and violent selves, having together killed over 100 million people!

After I got a copy of Hans's new book, I decided that the next move would be to write down what practically everyone thought was right and wrong. As you can see, Will, this was the exact opposite of what the violent ideologies had been trying to do—*force* their ideas of right and wrong on the world. We simply intensified our studies of ethics all across the world in all the religious and philosophical systems of the world both in the past and in the present. What we did was to consult—in writing and in person—all the experts in all these different systems—and soon in front of our eyes, we found certain basic ideas of what is right and wrong kept turning up in every system, every philosophy, and every religion! So, what we did was to try to write down as carefully and clearly as possible the ethical principles that we found were, in fact, common all across the world!

You might be thinking now, Will, that this list of the global ethical principles was going to be full of all kinds of familiar and strange religious languages. No, no, Will, we were deliberately very careful *not* to use any language that any group would find off-putting, and so, for example, there is no talk about God, or any quotations from the Qur'an, Bible, Vedas.... We chose language that *everybody* could say "yes" to.

Of course, there are lots of ethical principles that everybody will have which are *not* listed in this Global Ethic—only those ethical principles which *everybody* agrees on. However, there are lots of ethical decisions that everybody makes every day wherein there is disagreement—at times, even wide disagreement: Should we eat meat? Is homosexuality morally acceptable? Is abortion ever morally acceptable? Is socialism or capitalism morally the best system? ....

So you see, Will, there are many, many—a never-ending list of—ethical issues that we humans have to wrestle with, and new technologies will constantly bring us new ethical problems.

So, at the close of this letter about how we decide what is right and what is wrong, I hope that we have laid a foundation to begin to tackle these vital, never-ending ethical questions: Namely, the Golden Rule and the now slowly recognized Global Ethic.[2] But, we have only begun to scratch the surface.

Where do you think we should go from here? Your Opa would love to pick up on questions that are rattling around in your mind. Just drop me a line!

Liebe,

Opa

---

[2] See, for example, Leonard Swidler, Movement for a Global Ethic, *iPub Global Connection, LLC 2018*

Do Not Miss Out

Other Books in the Series

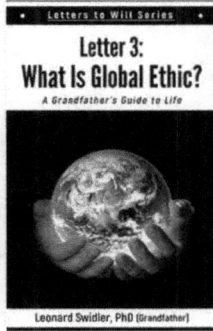